365 Affirmations for Black Women

Ignite Your Voice, Shatter Barriers, Cultivate Radiant Self-Love & Unstoppable Confidence

Mia Harper

PUBLISHING

Contents

A New Beginning

Welcome to a journey of empowerment, reflection, and growth—a journey that celebrates the depth, strength, and resilience of black women everywhere. "365 Affirmations for Black Women" is more than just a book; it is a daily invitation to embrace your story, to recognize your power, and to step into your light with confidence and grace.

In these pages, you'll find affirmations that speak to the heart of who we are—not just as individuals, but as a community. These words are crafted to uplift and inspire, to challenge and comfort, and to remind us of the unbreakable bond we share with one another.

As we move through each day, let's carry these affirmations with us as tools of empowerment and symbols of our collective journey. Let's use them to spark conversation, to build bridges, and to affirm our place in a world that so often tries to define us by its standards. Remember, it's not just about the heights we reach but about the journey we take and the sisters we uplift along the way.

This book is a testament to the power of voice—the power of your voice. It's an acknowledgment of our shared struggles and triumphs, our hopes and dreams, and the unyielding spirit that defines us. As we navigate the ups and downs of life, these affirmations are here to remind us that we are not alone, that our experiences are valid, and that our voices matter.

So, as you turn these pages, I invite you to embrace each affirmation with an open heart and an open mind. Let them be a source of strength on the difficult days and a beacon of joy on the good ones. Let them inspire you to live out loud, to love deeply, and to lead with courage and compassion.

Welcome to "365 Affirmations for Black Women." Welcome to a year of growth, empowerment, and unabashed self-love. Here's to us—bold, brilliant, and beautifully black.

Get ahead of the story: Scan to subscribe
and receive FREE early releases of ebooks
straight to your inbox!

January - Embracing New Beginnings with Hope and Grace

As we stand at the threshold of a new year, let's embrace the promise of fresh starts and new opportunities with open arms. This month is about setting intentions that reflect our highest aspirations for ourselves and for the communities we are a part of. Each day offers us a chance to begin anew, to redefine our paths, and to renew our commitment to living our lives with purpose and passion.

January 1: "Today, I step into the new year with an open heart, ready to embrace the endless possibilities that await me. I am grounded in my truth and propelled by my dreams."

January 2: "I acknowledge my strength and resilience, knowing that I have the power to overcome any challenge and turn obstacles into stepping stones."

January 3: "This day, I affirm my commitment to self-care and self-love, understanding that by nurturing myself, I am better equipped to serve those around me."

January 4: "I choose to see the beauty in my journey, celebrating each step, knowing that every experience enriches my life in profound ways."

January 5: "I embrace the power of my voice and my story. I speak my truth with confidence, knowing that my words have the power to inspire and effect change."

January 6: "With gratitude, I reflect on the lessons of the past, letting them inform but not define my future. I move forward with grace and wisdom."

January 7: "I open myself to new relationships and connections, recognizing the strength and support that lie in community and shared experiences."

January 8: "Today, I set boundaries with love and respect, honoring my needs and the integrity of my journey."

January 9: "I celebrate my unique talents and abilities, committing to use them in ways that bring joy to myself and others."

January 10: "In moments of doubt, I remind myself of my worth and the love that surrounds me, knowing that I am capable of achieving greatness."

January 11: "I honor the courage it takes to be true to myself. Today, I celebrate my authenticity and the peace it brings to my life."

January 12: "I am a gardener of my own life, planting seeds of success, happiness, and love that will grow into my future."

January 13: "In the quiet moments, I listen to my own needs, trusting in my ability to provide myself with care and compassion."

January 14: "I stand in my power, knowing that my journey influences others. Today, I lead by example, showing what it means to live with integrity and purpose."

January 15: "I embrace the diversity of my story, understanding that each chapter adds depth and value to who I am."

January 16: "Today, I choose to step out of my comfort zone, embracing the growth and opportunities that await me on the other side."

January 17: "I am surrounded by an abundance of love and support. I take a moment to acknowledge and appreciate the community that uplifts me."

January 18: "I give myself permission to dream boldly, setting goals that reflect my highest aspirations and deepest desires."

January 19: "I recognize the power of my decisions. Today, I make choices that align with my values and propel me toward my future."

January 20: "In the spirit of service, I remember that my actions can inspire and uplift others. I seek ways to contribute positively to my community."

January 21: "I celebrate the resilience that has brought me to this moment. My strength is a beacon of hope and a testament to my journey."

January 22: "I nurture my spirit with words of encouragement and acts of kindness, knowing that self-love is the foundation of my strength."

January 23: "Today, I reflect on the lessons learned from challenges faced, grateful for the growth and wisdom they have instilled in me."

January 24: "I am a creator of my own happiness. I pursue passions that fill my heart with joy and my life with purpose."

January 25: "I welcome change as a natural part of life, embracing the new paths it reveals with curiosity and optimism."

January 26: "I celebrate every victory, no matter the size, recognizing each as a step forward in my journey of growth and self-discovery."

January 27: "I am committed to living a life of balance, honoring both my work and my well-being with equal importance."

January 28: "I am open to the wisdom that comes with age and experience, seeing it as a gift that enriches my life in countless ways."

January 29: "I choose to face each day with gratitude, recognizing the beauty and blessings that surround me."

January 30: "I am a force of kindness and compassion in a world that needs it. Today, I spread love in ways both big and small."

January 31: "As January comes to a close, I look back with appreciation and forward with eager anticipation. I am ready for the chapters ahead, armed with hope, strength, and an unwavering belief in my potential."

HOPE AND GRACE REFLECTIONS JOURNAL

Reflect on the affirmations from the past month that centered on hope. Which specific affirmation resonated with you the most deeply, and why?

February - Cultivating Love and Self-Worth

As we step into February, let's turn our focus inward and to those we hold dear, dedicating this month to cultivating love and self-worth. This is a time for recognizing the love that begins within ourselves, and how it radiates outward, influencing all our relationships. It's about understanding our worth, embracing our value, and setting the standard for how we deserve to be treated.

February 1: "Today, I affirm my worthiness of love and respect. I recognize that self-love is the cornerstone of every relationship I build."

February 2: "I am deserving of love that is kind, honest, and supportive. I welcome relationships that uplift and empower me."

February 3: "I cherish my heart's capacity to love and be loved, acknowledging that vulnerability is a strength, not a weakness."

February 4: "I commit to treating myself with the same compassion and kindness that I offer to others, knowing that I am my first priority."

February 5: "I am a reflection of beauty, strength, and resilience. Today, I celebrate the love I have for myself and for the world around me."

February 6: "I acknowledge my worth and refuse to settle for less. My standards are a testament to my self-respect."

February 7: "In the journey of self-discovery, I honor my needs, my desires, and my dreams, making space for a love that truly fulfills me."

February 8: "I embrace the wisdom that comes from self-reflection, using it to guide my decisions in love and life."

February 9: "I am grateful for the love that surrounds me, from family, friends, and community. It is a reminder of the interconnectedness of our lives."

February 10: "I am a beacon of love and positivity, attracting relationships that mirror my commitment to growth and happiness."

February 11: "Today, I let go of relationships that do not honor my worth, making room for those that bring light and growth into my life."

February 12: "I celebrate the love that I am capable of giving and receiving, recognizing it as a true reflection of my inner beauty and strength."

February 13: "I am open to the lessons love teaches me, each one guiding me closer to understanding my true self and what I need to flourish."

February 14: "On this day of love, I honor my journey, acknowledging that every experience has prepared me for the love I rightly deserve."

February 15: "I affirm my independence and my ability to find fulfillment within myself, understanding that a partner complements, not completes me."

February 16: "I trust in the timing of my life, knowing that everything, including love, comes to me at the right moment and for the right reasons."

February 17: "I nurture the bonds that uplift and empower me, investing in relationships that are rooted in mutual respect and understanding."

February 18: "I am gentle with myself during times of heartache, allowing love's healing power to mend and strengthen my heart."

February 19: "I radiate confidence and self-assurance, attracting partners who respect and admire my strength and independence."

February 20: "I recognize the importance of setting boundaries, asserting them with kindness and clarity to protect my peace and well-being."

February 21: "I am thankful for the love that exists in my life, in all its forms, seeing it as a powerful force that connects and enriches us."

February 22: "I welcome growth within my relationships, embracing change as an opportunity to deepen connections and understanding."

February 23: "I celebrate my capacity for empathy and compassion, understanding that these qualities enhance my relationships and bring us closer."

February 24: "I am proud of the person I am becoming, a journey made possible by self-love, resilience, and the support of those who believe in me."

February 25: "I honor the love I have for myself, knowing it sets the foundation for all the love I give and receive in this world."

February 26: "I believe in the power of forgiveness, both of myself and others, recognizing it as a pathway to freedom and renewed love."

February 27: "I am a creator of joy and harmony in my relationships, fostering environments where love can thrive and blossom."

February 28: "I cherish the steps I've taken in love's journey, feeling prepared and hopeful for the future."

Leap Day, February 29: "I seize this rare day to shine with joy and journey forward with gratitude and grace."

LOVE AND SELF-WORTH INSIGHT JOURNAL

As you look forward to the next month, consider what aspects of love and self-worth you want to continue exploring or deepening. Craft a personal affirmation that encapsulates your goals or intentions related to these themes.

March - Embracing Empowerment

This month, we focus on empowerment—a force that drives us to realize our full potential and make impactful changes in our lives and the lives of those around us. Empowerment is about finding our voice, claiming our space, and standing up for what we believe in. It's about the courage to be authentically ourselves and the determination to pursue our goals with passion and perseverance.

March 1: "Today, I embrace my power to create change, both within myself and in the world around me. I am a force for good."

March 2: "I am empowered by my decisions and actions, knowing that I have the strength to overcome any obstacle that comes my way."

March 3: "I celebrate my unique talents and skills, understanding that they are gifts to be used in service of something greater than myself."

March 4: "I advocate for myself and others, using my voice to fight for justice, equality, and fairness in every space I occupy."

March 5: "I am committed to my personal growth, investing in my education and self-improvement as acts of empowerment."

March 6: "I recognize the power of community and solidarity, drawing strength from the collective courage of women who have paved the way."

March 7: "I stand firm in my values and beliefs, unwavering in the face of challenges and opposition."

March 8: "On International Women's Day, I honor the achievements of women worldwide and pledge to contribute to our shared progress."

March 9: "I am motivated by the successes of those who came before me, and I strive to be a role model for those who will follow."

March 10: "I nurture my inner leader, stepping forward with confidence to lead initiatives that inspire and uplift my community."

March 11: "I embrace the challenges that come my way, seeing them as opportunities to grow stronger and more resilient."

March 12: "I believe in my ability to make a difference. Today, I take one small step towards a big dream, knowing that every journey begins with a single step."

March 13: "I celebrate my independence, knowing that my freedom to make choices is a powerful tool in shaping my destiny."

March 14: "I am open to new perspectives and ideas, understanding that empowerment often comes from embracing the unknown."

March 15: "I am a beacon of encouragement and support for others, knowing that empowering those around me elevates us all."

March 16: "I prioritize my mental and emotional well-being, understanding that self-care is a radical act of empowerment."

March 17: "I stand in solidarity with those fighting for justice and equality, recognizing that our struggles and victories are interconnected."

March 18: "I celebrate my achievements, big and small, and recognize them as evidence of my capability and strength."

March 19: "I trust in my inner wisdom and intuition, guiding me towards choices that align with my true self."

March 20: "On the Spring Equinox, I welcome the renewal and growth that comes with the changing seasons, reflecting the evolution within myself."

March 21: "I am fearless in the pursuit of what sets my soul on fire, embracing passion as a source of power and purpose."

March 22: "I actively seek out opportunities for learning and growth, knowing that knowledge is a cornerstone of empowerment."

March 23: "I am gentle with myself during times of change, giving myself grace as I navigate the path of self-discovery and empowerment."

March 24: "I use my experiences, both good and bad, as stepping stones towards a future filled with promise and potential."

March 25: "I recognize the strength in vulnerability, allowing myself to be open and honest in my journey towards empowerment."

March 26: "I am a source of inspiration to myself and others, demonstrating that perseverance and determination can overcome any obstacle."

March 27: "I commit to acts of kindness and compassion, knowing they are powerful expressions of strength and empowerment."

March 28: "I am proud of who I am and who I am becoming, celebrating my journey with joy and anticipation for what is yet to come."

March 29: "I advocate for a balanced life, understanding that true empowerment means making space for work, play, and rest."

March 30: "I surround myself with positive influences, choosing relationships and environments that uplift and inspire me."

March 31: "As March ends, I reflect on the progress I've made and set my sights on new goals, ready to continue my journey of empowerment with hope and determination."

EMPOWERMENT REFLECTIONS JOURNAL

Reflect on a challenge you encountered this month. How did the theme of empowerment help you address or overcome this challenge? Which affirmation gave you the courage or confidence to persevere, and what did you learn about your resilience?

April - Cultivating Growth and Resilience

April brings with it the promise of renewal and the beauty of transformation. This month, we focus on cultivating growth and resilience, recognizing that the journey of self-improvement is both challenging and rewarding. Inspired by the strength and grace with which we navigate life's changes, these affirmations are a call to embrace our potential for growth and the resilience that lies within each of us.

April 1: "Today, I plant seeds of growth and change, nurturing them with hope, hard work, and dedication to bloom into their fullest potential."

April 2: "I welcome the challenges that come my way, knowing that each one is an opportunity to strengthen my resilience and character."

April 3: "I am committed to my personal development, embracing learning and growth as lifelong journeys."

April 4: "I find strength in my struggles, understanding that resilience is built through overcoming adversity."

April 5: "I celebrate the small victories, understanding that progress, no matter how small, is a step forward in my growth."

April 6: "I am adaptable and flexible, willing to change course when necessary to align with my goals and values."

April 7: "I trust in my ability to recover from setbacks, using them as a foundation for future success."

April 8: "I nurture my spirit with kindness and patience, knowing that growth is a process that requires time and care."

April 9: "I am open to new experiences and perspectives, understanding that they enrich my journey and contribute to my growth."

April 10: "I draw inspiration from the natural world, which teaches me about resilience and renewal in the face of change."

April 11: "Today, I remind myself that every experience, whether easy or challenging, contributes to my larger story of growth and resilience."

April 12: "I honor my journey, acknowledging that true growth often happens outside of my comfort zone."

April 13: "I am a testament to the power of perseverance, facing each day with courage and an unwavering belief in my ability to succeed."

April 14: "I cultivate patience, recognizing that some of life's most valuable lessons unfold over time, not overnight."

April 15: "I embrace my evolving self, celebrating the person I am today and the one I am becoming through my dedication to growth."

April 16: "I am resilient in the face of adversity, finding new ways to rise every time I am challenged."

April 17: "I focus on the progress I've made, understanding that each step forward enriches my journey and strengthens my spirit."

April 18: "I welcome feedback and constructive criticism, seeing them as opportunities to learn, adapt, and grow."

April 19: "I am rooted in my values and beliefs, yet flexible in my approach, allowing me to navigate life's changes with grace and wisdom."

April 20: "I recognize the strength within me, a force that propels me through challenges and towards my dreams with confidence."

April 21: "Today, I celebrate the beauty of becoming, knowing that each phase of my journey is a chapter in my story of resilience."

April 22: "On Earth Day, I am reminded of the resilience of nature and inspired to incorporate its lessons into my own growth and renewal."

April 23: "I am committed to self-reflection, understanding that looking inward is a crucial step in the journey of personal growth."

April 24: "I allow myself to let go of past mistakes, embracing forgiveness as a pathway to healing and growth."

April 25: "I seek out moments of joy and inspiration, knowing they fuel my resilience and capacity for growth."

April 26: "I am mindful of my mental and emotional well-being, understanding that resilience is also about knowing when to rest and recharge."

April 27: "I strive for balance, recognizing that growth involves harmonizing different aspects of my life—work, family, and self-care."

April 28: "I am empowered by my choices, knowing that each decision I make is a step towards a future I am actively shaping."

April 29: "I cherish my support network, grateful for the encouragement and strength I draw from those around me."

April 30: "As April concludes, I reflect on my growth with gratitude and look forward to the journey ahead, ready to embrace the lessons and opportunities that await."

GROWTH AND RESILIENCE REFLECTIONS JOURNAL

Reflect on how your journey of growth and resilience has impacted those around you. Is there a particular affirmation that not only empowered you but also inspired you to support others in their growth or resilience journey?

May - Embracing Joy and Happiness

As the warmth of May envelops us, let's turn our focus to the joy and happiness that enrich our lives. This month is about acknowledging the sources of our joy, actively seeking out happiness, and making space for the things and people that light up our world. Inspired by the laughter, and warmth of our community, these affirmations encourage us to connect with our joy and share it with others.

May 1: "Today, I choose to focus on the positives in my life, allowing them to lift my spirits and fill my heart with joy."

May 2: "I embrace the simple pleasures that bring me happiness, recognizing that often, joy is found in the smallest moments."

May 3: "I am grateful for the love and laughter that surround me, cherishing the connections that bring warmth to my days."

May 4: "I commit to pursuing my passions, knowing that following my heart is a direct path to true happiness."

May 5: "I celebrate my achievements and the journey that led me here, recognizing that happiness is found in both the pursuit and the accomplishment."

May 6: "I spread joy wherever I go, understanding that happiness shared is happiness multiplied."

May 7: "I take time to appreciate the beauty in the world around me, allowing it to inspire wonder and contentment in my heart."

May 8: "I nurture relationships that bring me happiness, investing in the community and connections that support and uplift me."

May 9: "I find strength in joy, using it as a source of energy and resilience through all of life's ups and downs."

May 10: "I allow myself to dream big, fueling my ambitions with the happiness that comes from pursuing what I love."

May 11: "I remind myself that happiness is a personal journey, unique to each of us, and I honor my path with kindness and patience."

May 12: "I recognize laughter as a healing force, seeking moments of joy and humor to lighten my heart and brighten my day."

May 13: "I cherish the gift of now, embracing the present moment fully, and finding joy in the here and now."

May 14: "I am open to new experiences that bring joy and excitement, understanding that growth often accompanies the pursuit of happiness."

May 15: "I express gratitude daily, knowing that appreciation for what I have brings contentment and multiplies my happiness."

May 16: "I cultivate a positive mindset, focusing on hopeful outcomes and the good in others, to attract more happiness into my life."

May 17: "I am mindful of my energy and the company I keep, surrounding myself with positivity and people who uplift me."

May 18: "I invest in my passions and hobbies, as they are essential sources of joy and fulfillment in my life."

May 19: "I take action towards creating the life I desire, knowing that happiness is often a result of living authentically and purposefully."

May 20: "I celebrate the diversity of joy in my life, recognizing that happiness comes in many forms and expressions."

May 21: "I foster an environment of joy within my home, making it a sanctuary of peace, love, and happiness."

May 22: "I acknowledge the role of challenges in cultivating depth and resilience, finding joy in overcoming them."

May 23: "I share my joy with others, knowing that in giving happiness, I also receive it."

May 24: "I embrace change with a joyful heart, trusting that new beginnings bring new opportunities for happiness."

May 25: "I honor my emotions, allowing myself to feel deeply, for in every emotion there's a potential for understanding and joy."

May 26: "I am thankful for the journey of life, with its highs and lows, for it teaches me to appreciate the moments of true happiness."

May 27: "I seek balance in my life, understanding that joy is found not in perpetual happiness but in living fully and meaningfully."

May 28: "I encourage others to pursue their happiness, supporting them in their journey towards joy and fulfillment."

May 29: "I reflect on the memories that bring me joy, using them as a beacon of light and inspiration in my life."

May 30: "I welcome the summer with an open heart, ready to embrace the warmth, light, and happiness it brings."

May 31: "As May concludes, I look back with gratitude for the moments of joy experienced and forward with anticipation for more to come."

JOY AND HAPPINESS REFLECTIONS JOURNAL

Reflect on the past month and think about a moment when you found joy in an unexpected place or situation. What was happening, and why did it bring you joy?

June - Nurturing Health and Wellness

In June, as we welcome the warmth and vitality of summer, our focus shifts to nurturing our health and wellness. This month is about honoring our bodies through movement, nourishing ourselves with foods that fuel us, and taking the time to rest and rejuvenate our minds and spirits. Inspired by the goal of a balanced, healthy lifestyle, these affirmations encourage us to commit to our well-being, understanding that self-care is a profound act of self-love.

June 1: "Today, I commit to making choices that honor my body and mind, understanding that my health is the foundation of my strength and happiness."

June 2: "I appreciate the incredible capabilities of my body and pledge to support it with exercise, rest, and nourishment."

June 3: "I prioritize my mental health, seeking activities and practices that bring me peace, clarity, and emotional balance."

June 4: "I embrace the healing power of nature, spending time outdoors to rejuvenate my spirit and connect with the world around me."

June 5: "I listen to my body's needs, resting when I need to rest and moving when I need to move, in a beautiful dance of self-care."

June 6: "I nourish my body with foods that are good for me, enjoying the flavors and the energy they bring to my life."

June 7: "I practice mindfulness and gratitude, recognizing that a healthy mind contributes to a healthy body and a joyful heart."

June 8: "I explore new ways to stay active, finding joy in the movement and strength in the challenge."

June 9: "I am gentle with myself, understanding that wellness is a journey with ups and downs, and compassion is key."

June 10: "I celebrate each step I take towards a healthier lifestyle, knowing that every positive choice is a victory."

June 11: "I seek balance in all aspects of my life, recognizing that wellness involves both action and rest, speaking and silence, giving and receiving."

June 12: "Today, I honor my journey towards wellness, understanding that each person's path is unique and deserving of respect and empathy."

June 13: "I cultivate a supportive community around health and wellness, sharing my journey and learning from the experiences of others."

June 14: "I embrace self-care as a vital practice, scheduling time for activities that replenish my energy and bring me joy."

June 15: "I acknowledge my progress, no matter how small, understanding that wellness is a series of small choices that add up to significant change."

June 16: "I integrate mindfulness into my daily routine, allowing myself moments of quiet reflection to nurture peace within."

June 17: "I celebrate the diversity of ways to achieve health and wellness, exploring various practices and embracing what works best for me."

June 18: "I am thankful for the ability to move and be active, and I seek out physical activities that I enjoy and that inspire me to continue."

June 19: "On Juneteenth, I reflect on the resilience and strength of my ancestors, drawing inspiration from their journey towards freedom and well-being."

June 20: "I welcome the summer solstice by setting intentions for health and happiness, embracing the light and warmth that the season brings."

June 21: "I practice kindness and compassion towards myself, especially on days when I feel less than my best, knowing that wellness includes grace and understanding."

June 22: "I focus on hydration and the simple act of drinking water, appreciating it as a fundamental yet powerful form of self-care."

June 23: "I explore the healing arts, such as meditation, yoga, or tai chi, embracing their benefits for both mind and body."

June 24: "I make time for laughter and play, recognizing these as essential elements of a well-rounded and joyful life."

June 25: "I honor my need for sleep and rest, understanding that rejuvenation is a cornerstone of health and vitality."

June 26: "I reflect on my emotional well-being, engaging in practices that promote emotional intelligence and resilience."

June 27: "I acknowledge the power of food as medicine, choosing nutrients that support my body's needs and enhance my overall well-being."

June 28: "I cherish connections with loved ones, knowing that strong relationships contribute to my emotional and mental health."

June 29: "I give myself permission to do nothing at all, understanding that sometimes, stillness is the best form of self-care."

June 30: "As June comes to a close, I reflect on the wellness journey I've embarked upon, feeling grateful for the growth and insights gained, and eager for the continuous journey ahead."

Health and Wellness Insight Journal

Consider a moment this month when you felt a strong connection between your mental and physical well-being. How did your emotional state impact your physical health, or vice versa?

July - Harnessing Strength and Courage

In July, as we stand in the full blaze of summer, we turn our attention to the themes of strength and courage. This month is a tribute to our inner fortitude, the bravery we muster in the face of life's challenges, and the unwavering spirit that propels us forward. These affirmations encourage us to embrace our strength, confront our fears, and walk our paths with courage.

July 1: "Today, I affirm my strength is greater than any challenge I may face. I am equipped with resilience and courage."

July 2: "I stand tall in the face of adversity, drawing on the well of courage that resides within me."

July 3: "I embrace my power to make a difference, stepping forward with bravery to effect change in my life and community."

July 4: "On this day of independence, I celebrate my freedom to choose my path, courageously pursuing my dreams and goals."

July 5: "I confront my fears head-on, understanding that courage is not the absence of fear, but the determination to move forward despite it."

July 6: "I draw strength from my past experiences, knowing that each has prepared me to face the future with confidence."

July 7: "I am resilient, bouncing back from setbacks with greater wisdom and strength."

July 8: "I trust in my abilities and make decisions with confidence, knowing that I am capable of overcoming obstacles."

July 9: "I practice self-compassion, understanding that being gentle with myself in times of struggle is a form of strength."

July 10: "I am motivated by the courage of those who came before me, using their examples to fuel my own journey of empowerment."

July 11: "I celebrate my victories, both big and small, recognizing each as a testament to my strength and perseverance."

July 12: "I nurture my spirit with positive thoughts and actions, knowing that a strong mind leads to a strong life."

July 13: "I am a warrior in my own life, bravely battling against doubt and fear to create a future filled with hope and possibility."

July 14: "I allow myself to be vulnerable, understanding that true courage involves opening up to both risks and rewards."

July 15: "I am steadfast in my commitments, pushing through challenges with unwavering determination and focus."

July 16: "I seek out and embrace opportunities for growth, knowing that stepping out of my comfort zone builds strength and character."

July 17: "I am resilient, transforming every obstacle into a stepping stone towards my success and happiness."

July 18: "I empower myself through education and learning, fortifying my mind with knowledge that builds confidence and courage."

July 19: "I support and uplift others, sharing my strength in a way that encourages them to embrace their own power and potential."

July 20: "I am anchored by my values and principles, which guide me through life's storms with courage and integrity."

July 21: "I face the unknown with optimism and bravery, excited by the possibilities that lie ahead, ready to navigate them with grace."

July 22: "I celebrate the diversity of my strengths, recognizing that each contributes uniquely to my ability to face life's challenges."

July 23: "I am confident in my ability to resolve conflicts and face difficult situations, approaching them with wisdom and courage."

July 24: "I honor the journey of others, learning from their stories of strength and resilience, inspired to cultivate the same within myself."

July 25: "I maintain a hopeful outlook, believing in my capacity to overcome and thrive, no matter what life throws my way."

July 26: "I am a beacon of courage for those around me, demonstrating that strength is not just what we carry but what we share."

July 27: "I embrace change as an opportunity for growth, facing it with a brave heart and an open mind, ready for transformation."

July 28: "I give myself the gift of forgiveness, understanding that releasing past hurts is a powerful act of strength and renewal."

July 29: "I balance strength with gentleness, knowing that true power lies in the ability to navigate life with both firmness and kindness."

July 30: "I am grateful for my body's strength and what it allows me to accomplish, treating it with care and respect as a temple of my spirit."

July 31: "As July closes, I reflect on the strength I've shown and the courage I've harnessed, feeling prepared and energized for the adventures that await."

STRENGTH AND COURAGE REFLECTIONS JOURNAL

Think back over the past month and identify a situation where you had to tap into your inner strength. What was the challenge, and how did you confront it?

_____

_____

_____

_____

_____

_____

_____

_____

_____

_____

_____

_____

_____

_____

_____

_____

_____

_____

_____

_____

AUGUST - EMBRACING REFLECTION AND SELF-DISCOVERY

August's warmth invites us to slow down and turn inward, making it the perfect time for reflection and self-discovery. This month, we will get inspired to explore our journey of understanding ourselves, our values, and our aspirations. These affirmations are designed to encourage introspection, celebrate our unique paths, and foster a deeper connection with our true selves.

August 1: "Today, I give myself permission to pause and reflect, understanding that self-discovery is a vital step towards living authentically."

August 2: "I embrace my story, including every high and low, recognizing that each experience has shaped me into who I am today."

August 3: "I am open to exploring my inner world, curious about the dreams, desires, and values that drive me."

August 4: "I celebrate my uniqueness, understanding that my individual journey adds valuable perspective and richness to the world."

August 5: "I listen to my intuition, trusting it as a guide towards choices that align with my true self."

August 6: "I honor my growth and transformation, recognizing that change is a natural and necessary part of life."

August 7: "I am patient with myself in moments of uncertainty, knowing that clarity comes with time and reflection."

August 8: "I value my alone time, seeing it as an opportunity to connect deeply with myself and recharge."

August 9: "I am committed to understanding my needs and boundaries, communicating them with confidence and clarity."

August 10: "I explore new interests and passions, allowing myself the freedom to evolve and discover new aspects of myself."

August 11: "I reflect on the relationships in my life, appreciating those that bring positivity and growth, and reevaluating those that do not serve my well-being."

August 12: "I acknowledge my fears and face them with courage, understanding that overcoming them is a significant part of self-discovery."

August 13: "I give myself the space to dream without limits, exploring the possibilities of what my life can become."

August 14: "I am gentle with myself during times of inner turmoil, knowing that self-compassion is key to navigating the journey of self-discovery."

August 15: "I celebrate my progress, no matter how small, recognizing that every step forward is a victory in my journey of personal growth."

August 16: "I engage in activities that nourish my soul, understanding that happiness and fulfillment come from aligning with my passions and interests."

August 17: "I take time to write down my thoughts and reflections, finding clarity and insight through the process of journaling."

August 18: "I seek wisdom from my experiences, using them as lessons to guide my future decisions and actions."

August 19: "I am mindful of the words I speak to myself, choosing affirmations and thoughts that uplift and motivate me."

August 20: "I embrace the unknown with optimism, seeing the potential for growth and new experiences as exciting opportunities."

August 21: "I honor my past, present, and future, understanding that each phase of my life holds its own beauty and significance."

August 22: "I cultivate a sense of inner peace, finding ways to center and ground myself amidst life's inevitable changes."

August 23: "I recognize the power of my choices, committing to decisions that reflect my values, hopes, and dreams."

August 24: "I appreciate the complexity of my emotions, allowing myself to feel deeply and express my feelings authentically."

August 25: "I explore the arts as a pathway to understanding myself better, whether through music, painting, writing, or dance."

August 26: "I practice gratitude, acknowledging the blessings in my life and the journey that has led me to where I am."

August 27: "I am curious about the world around me, understanding that external exploration can spark internal revelation."

August 28: "I commit to lifelong learning, embracing new knowledge and experiences as tools for self-improvement and enlightenment."

August 29: "I value quiet moments of meditation or prayer, using them as opportunities to connect with my inner self and higher power."

August 30: "I envision the person I aim to become, setting intentions and goals that align with my deepest desires and values."

August 31: "As August concludes, I reflect on the insights gained and the growth experienced, feeling grateful for the journey of self-discovery and the paths yet to explore."

REFLECTION AND SELF-DISCOVERY JOURNAL

Self-discovery often involves exploring our inner landscapes and uncovering hidden aspects of ourselves. Reflect on an aspect of yourself that you discovered or began to understand more deeply this month.

September - Creating Balance and Harmony

As the seasons transition from the warmth of summer to the mellow tones of autumn, September calls us to seek balance and harmony in our lives; to balance personal, professional, and public life with grace, these affirmations encourage us to find our own equilibrium, ensuring that we nurture all aspects of our being for overall well-being and fulfillment.

September 1: "Today, I embrace the art of balance, recognizing that my well-being depends on nurturing both my inner self and my external responsibilities."

September 2: "I seek harmony in my daily routine, finding a rhythm that allows me to flow between my duties and my desires with ease and joy."

September 3: "I prioritize my mental and physical health, understanding that maintaining balance is key to my strength and resilience."

September 4: "I cultivate peace within my heart and mind, allowing this inner tranquility to influence my surroundings and relationships."

September 5: "I practice the balance of giving and receiving, understanding that both are necessary for a fulfilling and harmonious life."

September 6: "I strive for equilibrium in my professional and personal life, ensuring that neither is neglected at the expense of the other."

September 7: "I allow myself moments of rest and reflection, recognizing that quietude is essential for maintaining balance and harmony."

September 8: "I embrace flexibility in my plans and expectations, adapting with grace to life's ever-changing dynamics."

September 9: "I nurture my relationships with care and attention, valuing the harmony that comes from mutual respect and understanding."

September 10: "I set boundaries with kindness and firmness, protecting my energy and well-being as I engage with the world around me."

September 11: "I find strength in the balance between speaking my truth and listening to others, valuing the harmony that respectful dialogue can bring."

September 12: "I dedicate time to my hobbies and interests, recognizing that personal fulfillment is a crucial element of a balanced life."

September 13: "I appreciate the moments of stillness in my day, understanding that silence can be a powerful source of balance and renewal."

September 14: "I manage my time with intention, allocating moments for work, play, and rest, ensuring a harmonious blend of productivity and relaxation."

September 15: "I honor the balance between independence and seeking support, knowing that both are necessary for a healthy and harmonious life."

September 16: "I celebrate the balance in nature, drawing inspiration from its effortless harmony to guide my own life towards equilibrium."

September 17: "I embrace the journey towards balance, accepting that it is a continuous process of adjustment and alignment with my core values."

September 18: "I seek harmony in my physical environment, creating spaces that reflect tranquility and promote well-being."

September 19: "I balance my aspirations with gratitude for the present moment, finding joy in the journey as much as in the destination."

September 20: "I navigate life's challenges with a balanced perspective, focusing on solutions that bring peace and positive outcomes."

September 21: "I encourage a harmonious blend of tradition and innovation in my life, respecting the past while embracing the future."

September 22: "On the Autumn Equinox, I reflect on the balance of light and darkness, celebrating the transitions that bring growth and change."

September 23: "I foster balanced relationships, where give-and-take, respect, and mutual growth are foundational principles."

September 24: "I cultivate inner harmony by aligning my thoughts, words, and actions with my highest intentions and values."

September 25: "I balance my need for security with the courage to take risks, understanding that both are essential for a fulfilling life."

September 26: "I cherish the balance between community involvement and personal solitude, recognizing the value of both in my life."

September 27: "I practice financial balance, managing my resources wisely to support both my current needs and future dreams."

September 28: "I seek balance in my emotional life, allowing myself to feel deeply while maintaining resilience and poise."

September 29: "I honor the balance of learning and teaching, understanding that in every exchange, there is an opportunity to grow and contribute."

September 30: "As September ends, I reflect on the harmony achieved and the lessons learned, grateful for the balance that guides my path forward."

BALANCE AND HARMONY JOURNAL

Reflect on a day or moment from the past month that felt perfectly balanced. What elements (work, leisure, relationships, self-care, etc.) were in harmony, and how did you achieve this balance?

OCTOBER - EMBRACING TRANSFORMATION

As the leaves change color and fall, October reminds us of the beauty and inevitability of change. This month, we will find inspiration for a journey of continuous growth and transformation, we focus on embracing the changes within us and around us. These affirmations are crafted to encourage self-reflection, celebrate growth, and welcome the transformative power of embracing new beginnings.

October 1: "Today, I open my heart to change, seeing it as an opportunity for growth and a pathway to discovering my true potential."

October 2: "I welcome transformation in my life, understanding that each change brings me closer to the person I aspire to be."

October 3: "I embrace the process of becoming, knowing that personal evolution involves both challenges and triumphs."

October 4: "I celebrate my journey of transformation, recognizing that every experience has contributed to my growth."

October 5: "I am flexible and adaptable, willing to adjust my path as I learn and grow through life's varied experiences."

October 6: "I trust in the timing of my life, understanding that transformation cannot be rushed but unfolds in its own perfect timing."

October 7: "I seek lessons in every change, viewing obstacles as opportunities to strengthen and refine my character."

October 8: "I honor my past as the foundation of my future, grateful for the experiences that have shaped me and excited for those yet to come."

October 9: "I cultivate a mindset open to new possibilities, ready to embrace the unknown with curiosity and optimism."

October 10: "I acknowledge my fears of change, facing them with courage and the belief that I am capable of navigating any transition."

October 11: "I nurture my resilience, understanding that it is through embracing change that I build strength and flexibility."

October 12: "I reflect on my achievements, seeing them as milestones in my journey of transformation and signs of my capacity to evolve."

October 13: "I welcome new perspectives and ideas, recognizing that transformation often begins with a shift in mindset."

October 14: "I give myself permission to let go of what no longer serves me, making space for new growth and opportunities."

October 15: "I am patient with myself during periods of transition, knowing that great changes are often preceded by chaos and uncertainty."

October 16: "I cherish my relationships, understanding that as I transform, so too may my connections with others, growing in depth and understanding."

October 17: "I engage with my passions and curiosities, allowing them to guide me toward new paths and expressions of self."

October 18: "I practice gratitude for the journey, acknowledging that every step of my transformation is worth celebrating."

October 19: "I am committed to my personal growth, dedicating time each day to activities that enrich my soul and expand my horizons."

October 20: "I find courage in my community, drawing strength from shared experiences and mutual support during times of change."

October 21: "I recognize the beauty in my evolving story, viewing each chapter as an essential part of my unique journey."

October 22: "I embrace the seasonal shift as a mirror of my own changes, finding harmony with nature's cycles of growth and renewal."

October 23: "I focus on the present, mindful that living fully in each moment is a powerful form of transformation."

October 24: "I envision the future with hope and excitement, inspired by the endless possibilities that await me."

October 25: "I balance reflection with action, understanding that thoughtful planning coupled with decisive movement propels me forward."

October 26: "I celebrate the diversity of my experiences, knowing that each has contributed to the rich tapestry of my life."

October 27: "I am gentle with my evolving self, embracing each new discovery with kindness and an open heart."

October 28: "I encourage others on their paths of transformation, sharing insights and support as we journey together."

October 29: "I acknowledge the strength it takes to change, honoring the courage within me and around me."

October 30: "I savor the quiet moments of introspection, finding in them the seeds of profound change and growth."

October 31: "As October ends, I look back on a month of transformation with gratitude, ready to welcome the next phase of my journey with open arms."

PERSONAL TRANSFORMATION INSIGHT JOURNAL

Transformation often occurs through overcoming challenges. Identify a challenge you faced this month that led to personal growth.

November -
Cultivating
Gratitude and
Giving

As the year begins to wind down and we enter the season of thanksgiving, November calls us to turn our hearts towards gratitude and generosity. These affirmations are designed to remind us of the importance of acknowledging our blessings and sharing our abundance with others.

November 1: "Today, I open my heart to gratitude, recognizing the abundance in my life and the many forms it takes."

November 2: "I express thanks for the people in my life, understanding that relationships are among the most precious gifts."

November 3: "I find ways to give back, knowing that generosity enriches both the giver and the receiver."

November 4: "I appreciate the simple joys of life, finding gratitude in moments of laughter, peace, and connection."

November 5: "I reflect on the challenges I've faced, grateful for the strength they've instilled in me and the growth they've spurred."

November 6: "I share my talents and resources with those in need, contributing to the well-being of my community and beyond."

November 7: "I cultivate a mindset of abundance, believing that there is enough for everyone and acting from a place of generosity."

November 8: "I acknowledge the beauty of nature and the environment, expressing gratitude for its sustenance and inspiration."

November 9: "I remember to thank myself, honoring the care, effort, and love I've invested in my journey."

November 10: "I practice daily gratitude, making it a habit to recognize and appreciate the blessings in my life."

November 11: "I cherish the act of giving, finding joy in the smiles and happiness of others, and knowing my actions make a difference."

November 12: "I take a moment to appreciate the educators, mentors, and guides who have illuminated my path with their wisdom and kindness."

November 13: "I practice gratitude not just in thought, but in action, by living each day with intention and kindness towards others."

November 14: "I am thankful for the gift of health, cherishing my body's strength and committing to caring for it with love and respect."

November 15: "I recognize the power of a grateful heart to transform challenges into opportunities for growth and connection."

November 16: "I extend my gratitude to the unseen hands that contribute to my comfort and well-being, from farmers to frontline workers."

November 17: "I make time to reconnect with nature, expressing my thankfulness for its beauty, resilience, and the peace it offers."

November 18: "I acknowledge the lessons learned from hardship, grateful for the resilience and insight each has brought into my life."

November 19: "I celebrate the diversity of life's experiences, understanding that each has contributed to the richness of my journey."

November 20: "I offer my support and compassion to those in need, recognizing that giving is one of the highest expressions of gratitude."

November 21: "I reflect on my personal growth over the year, grateful for the journey and the progress, no matter how small."

November 22: "I express my love and appreciation to my family and friends, understanding that these bonds are foundational to my happiness and success."

November 23: "I embrace the opportunity to start anew each day, thankful for the chance to live, learn, and love with fullness."

November 24: "On Thanksgiving, I gather with loved ones in spirit or in presence, celebrating our blessings and the abundance we share."

November 25: "I commit to carrying the spirit of gratitude beyond this month, letting it guide my actions and interactions every day."

November 26: "I find peace in the quiet moments of reflection, thankful for the journey of life and all it encompasses."

November 27: "I welcome the warmth and generosity of the holiday season, ready to spread cheer and kindness in abundance."

November 28: "I am grateful for the creativity and inspiration that flow through me, viewing each as a precious gift to be nurtured and shared."

November 29: "I honor the strength and courage within me and around me, thankful for the spirit of resilience that connects us all."

November 30: "As November ends, I look back with a heart full of gratitude, ready to embrace the final chapter of the year with hope and generosity."

GRATITUDE AND GIVING JOURNAL

Our relationships are fertile ground for practicing gratitude and giving. Reflect on a relationship that you're especially thankful for this month.

DECEMBER - EMBRACING REFLECTION AND CELEBRATION

As the year draws to a close and the festive spirit of December surrounds us, it's a time for reflection and celebration. We will practice looking back with gratitude and forward with hope, these affirmations are crafted to help us review our year's journey, honor our successes and challenges, and welcome the coming year with open hearts and renewed aspirations.

December 1: "Today, I begin the month of reflection, taking stock of my journey this year and acknowledging every step forward."

December 2: "I celebrate the strength I've found in moments of challenge, recognizing that each has contributed to my resilience and growth."

December 3: "I express gratitude for the love and support I've received, cherishing the connections that have enriched my life."

December 4: "I reflect on the moments of joy and laughter, understanding that these are the treasures that make life beautiful."

December 5: "I honor the lessons learned, viewing each as a stepping stone towards wisdom and a deeper understanding of myself."

December 6: "I take pride in my accomplishments, no matter how small, recognizing that progress is made up of small, consistent steps."

December 7: "I acknowledge the areas where I've struggled, seeing them as opportunities for learning and personal development."

December 8: "I embrace the spirit of the holiday season, spreading kindness, joy, and generosity in my community and beyond."

December 9: "I revisit my goals and dreams, celebrating the progress I've made and setting my sights on new horizons."

December 10: "I cultivate hope for the future, believing in the endless possibilities that await and my power to make them real."

December 11: "I find peace in the stillness of winter, using this time to rest, recharge, and reflect on the year's journey."

December 12: "I acknowledge the importance of self-care during the holiday season, ensuring that I nurture my well-being amidst the festivities."

December 13: "I share stories of the past year with loved ones, recognizing that our shared experiences strengthen our bonds."

December 14: "I embrace forgiveness, both giving and receiving, as a gift of the season, understanding its power to heal and renew."

December 15: "I delight in the tradition of giving, finding creative ways to express love and appreciation to those who matter most."

December 16: "I reserve moments for solitude and introspection, valuing the clarity and insight that come from quiet reflection."

December 17: "I celebrate the diversity of holiday traditions around the world, appreciating the rich tapestry of cultures that enrich our collective experience."

December 18: "I honor the memory of those no longer with us, holding them close in heart through cherished rituals and remembrances."

December 19: "I welcome the opportunity to set new intentions, viewing the coming year as a canvas for dreams, goals, and aspirations."

December 20: "I appreciate the beauty of the season, whether in the sparkle of holiday lights or the tranquility of a winter's night."

December 21: "On the Winter Solstice, I celebrate the return of light, embracing hope and the promise of brighter days ahead."

December 22: "I recognize the value of patience and waiting, seeing the period leading up to the new year as a time for grounding and preparation."

December 23: "I express my love through acts of kindness, understanding that the true spirit of the season is found in connection and generosity."

December 24: "On Christmas Eve, I cherish the magic of anticipation, enjoying the warmth and joy that comes from awaiting something wonderful."

December 25: "I celebrate the day with gratitude for the present moment, embracing the love, peace, and happiness that surround me."

December 26: "I reflect on the changes I wish to make, approaching self-improvement with compassion and a willingness to grow."

December 27: "I savor the quiet after the holiday rush, finding contentment in moments of simplicity and rest."

December 28: "I review the past year's resolutions, acknowledging my efforts and setting realistic, inspiring goals for the year to come."

December 29: "I connect with friends and family, sharing hopes and dreams for the future, and reinforcing the bonds that unite us."

December 30: "I give thanks for the year's lessons and blessings, ready to close this chapter with appreciation and grace."

December 31: "As the year concludes, I celebrate the journey, the growth, and the resilience I've shown, stepping into the new year empowered and hopeful."

CELEBRATION INSIGHTS JOURNAL

Reflect on a small victory you experienced this month and why it felt significant to you. What affirmation helped you recognize and celebrate this achievement?

Afterword - A Year of Growth, Empowerment, and Gratitude

As we come to the close of this journey together, it's a moment to pause and reflect on the journey we've undertaken. "365 Affirmations for Black Women" was crafted to be more than just a book; it was intended as a daily companion to guide you through a year of self-discovery, growth, and empowerment. We've traversed themes that touch upon the essence of what it means to live fully, from embracing our strength and resilience to cultivating gratitude and generosity.

Throughout the year, you've been invited to reflect on your journey, celebrate your achievements, and embrace your challenges as opportunities for growth. Each month's theme was carefully chosen to mirror the seasons of the year and the seasons of life, recognizing that just as nature cycles through phases of growth, decay, and renewal, so too do we.

Reflecting on Our Journey

This book has been a space for reflection, offering affirmations that encourage you to pause, consider your path, and appreciate the beauty of your journey. It has also been a source of empowerment, providing words of encouragement and motivation to lift you up, remind you of your strength, and inspire you to claim your space in the world with confidence and grace.

Celebrating Growth and Resilience

Each affirmation was a celebration of your inherent worth, your resilience in the face of adversity, and your capacity for love and joy. You were encouraged to acknowledge your growth, to honor your struggles, and to cherish the moments of triumph, no matter how small.

Looking Forward with Hope

As we look forward to the days ahead, let the lessons and affirmations in this book serve as foundations upon which to build. Let them remind you of your power to effect change in your life and the lives of those around you. Let them inspire you to continue on your path of self-discovery, armed with the knowledge that you are capable of overcoming any obstacle and achieving your deepest desires.

A Final Word of Gratitude

Thank you for allowing this book to be a part of your journey. It is my hope that these affirmations have brought you comfort, inspiration, and a deeper connection to the incredible strength and beauty that lies within you. Remember, your journey is uniquely yours, but you are never alone. May you step into each new day with confidence, grace, and an open heart, ready to embrace all the joy, challenges, and opportunities that life has to offer.

Here's to a future filled with growth, empowerment, and endless possibilities. May you always find strength in your roots, light in your path, and love in your journey.

With gratitude and best wishes,

Mia Harper

Made in United States
Orlando, FL
15 November 2024